Earthly Days

Printed in the United States of America

ISBN 979-8-89114-005-9 (sc)
ISBN 979-8-89114-006-6 (e)

Library of Congress Control Number: 2023913525

2023.07.31

MainSpring Books
5901 W. Century Blvd
Suite 750
Los Angeles, CA, US, 90045

www.mainspringbooks.com

Earthly Days

POEMS BY

CHERYL BATAVIA

Dedication

Dedicated with love
to my soulmate,

Robert Snyder

Preface

In retirement, I look back over my life with its full measure of opportunities and challenges. Life has been, and continues to be, an adventure!

Reflecting on my experiences, whatever meaning I find, I endeavor to share through my poems. I hope you enjoy reading *Earthly Days*; may your days on Earth be blissful!

Acknowledgements

At the beginning of the pandemic, encouraged by Kritika, a young poet from India who found my website, I started a poetry blog on WordPress.

Blogging was the perfect antidote to the isolation of the pandemic and continues to enhance my life. WordPress bloggers learn from, inspire, and encourage each other.

Thank you to my children for your ongoing love and support. I am so proud of you!

Yolanda, it means a lot to me to have a sister to talk with about our shared history and the experiences of daily life.

Thank you, Robert, for all the thoughtful, supportive things you do every day. It is my honor and privilege to spend our retirement years together.

Thank you to my advisor, Christopher Hernandez, the designer, A.C. Young, the production team, and all the talented people at Mainspring Press who made this book a reality.

Contents

NOSTALGIA

MOTHER NATURE

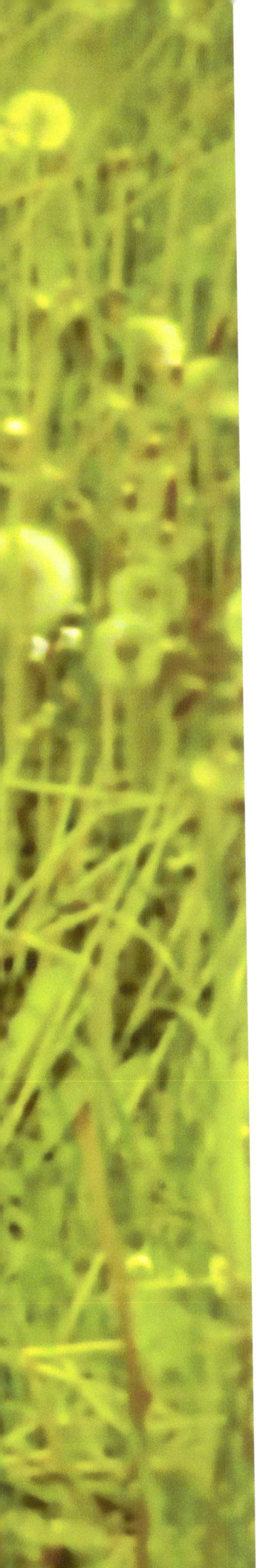

PERSPECTIVES

Transitions

As vapor in clouds
condenses into rain,
so may I adapt.

As wind carries seeds
to faraway locations,
so may I move forward.

As soil welcomes seeds,
so may my mind
be receptive to new ideas.

May sunshine relentlessly
enlighten me, mind and soul!

Identity Crisis

Purpose of life?
Distraction banishes purpose.
Here am I.
Who am I? Why am I?
Anxiety overpowers curiosity.
Why contemplate?
I stand at the crossroads of my unexamined life.
Contemplate why!
Curiosity overpowers anxiety.
I am here.
I am why! I am who!
Purpose banishes distraction...
Life of purpose.

Abracadabra!

Questions work magic!
Great discoveries appear
when we seek answers.

Egalitarian Utopia

All human beings,
individual, unique,
nurture their talents...
equals working together
to create a better world.

This Little Boat

Courage, friend, as onward we go!
If you keep on bailing as I row,
we may reach the shore, I think,
before our little boat has time to sink.

Among Friends

Day-by-day, we live on Earth.
Face-to-face or virtually, we greet each other.
Eye-to-eye, we often see.
Toe-to-toe, we engage in friendly competition.
Side-by-side, we work together.
Arm-in-arm, we walk along.
Hand-in-hand, we share life's journey.
Moment-by-moment, we face life's uncertainties.
Heart-to-heart, we know we are not alone.

Flimflam World

The longer you live, the more crooks you will find
bound and determined to rob you blind!
They do so many things that just aren't right,
which makes me wonder...How can they sleep at night,
these con artists, schemers and scammers,
charlatans, and flimflammers?

The world is crawling with dirty dealers,
false advertisers, chiselers, and cheaters.
Swindlers make promises too good to be true.
Fly-by-night tradesmen are targeting you.
Annoying junk mail and phone soliciters
are high-pressure hucksters and time wasters.

There's no end in sight for white-collar crime,
fakers and phishers, identity thieves online,
snake oil salesmen, online quacks,
weight loss gurus, and computer hackers.
Dressed for success are those insider traders,
predatory lenders, and pension fund raiders.

On social media, conspiracy theories confuse.
Questionable sources proclaim, "Fake news!"
Who can we trust to make criminals stop?
Not corrupt politicians or crooked cops!
With so many people who intend to deceive,
how can we ever know what to believe?

My suggestion of the place to start:
Make sure you, yourself, are pure in heart!
Do an honest day's work, treat others fairly,
and set an example of honor and integrity.
Don't value leaders above ethical beliefs...
Charismatic leaders may be liars and thieves.

Don't believe everything you read or hear!
Consider all options until the issues are clear.
Avoid anything that seems too good to be true.
"Trust but verify!" is a motto to pursue.
Crooks are vastly outnumbered by honest folks.
Believe in yourself, and don't give up hope!

No Time for Fears

I choose
to assess risks and act judiciously.
I choose never to live in fear, to live joyously,
sleep soundly, and focus on my goals.
I have no time for fears!

Message in a Bottle

A barefoot wanderer on the sands of time,
moment-to-moment, no reason or rhyme,
searching for a message in a bottle along the shoreline,
but pebbles on the beach were all I could find.

Looking for the light of my life, year after year,
I sang along with the music of the spheres,
seeking someone to sing with me as we embark,
two-by-two onto an archetypical ark.

I rowed my small boat...On dry land, I planted my feet.
Miracle of miracles, soon we were dancing cheek-to-cheek!
All was bright where once were darkness and strife.
I smiled at you, the love of my life!

From each rising sun to the next rising sun,
on top of the world, under the gun,
or tossed by capricious seas, we've had a good run.
We've sailed life together, and it's been fun!

Hand-in-hand on the beach, we walk once more;
a message in a bottle washes up on the shore.
With hearts aflutter and chaos of mind,
we uncork the bottle, unsettled by what we find.

With the music of the spheres, our hearts are in tune,
but the message in the bottle portends impending doom.
It says, "Tis a short voyage from cradle to tomb."
We face an epic tidal wave...The end has come so soon!

I Am the Moment

I am that flash of green as the sun goes down.
I am the crest of a wave before it breaks on the shore,
a lightning bolt that ushers in a clap of thunder.

I am the moment of a butterfly's first flight,
the rush of sea turtle hatchlings to the safety of the sea.
I am the moment when lover's eyes first meet.

I am that half-forgotten melody that lingers in your mind,
a half-remembered dream that eludes you when you wake.
I am that pang of regret for a kind word left unspoken.

I am the blink of an eye, the shadow of a smile.
I am that pivotal moment when opportunity knocks.
I am the moment...and then I am gone.

LOVE

Summer Rain

We laughed in the rain
as we walked to the oak tree
half a century ago.

Stolen kiss in summer rain...
I hope life's been good to you!

Just the Two of Us

One day we made the winding, steep descent,
enchanted by the waterfall's sweet song.
In pools below, we swam to heart's content,
the two of us together all day long.

One day we climbed up to the mountaintop,
where winter winds had dwarfed the ancient trees,
where we lay dreaming on a sun-warmed rock,
our skin caressed by every summer breeze.

One day we strolled among the ferns so green,
a fragrant carpet on the forest floor.
Below us stretched a peaceful valley scene.
We thought our love would last forevermore.

Oh, those were golden days I spent with you,
enjoying nature's wonders, just we two.

Great Discoveries of Love

Like Galileo viewing stars and planets
through his telescope,
we see the light in each other's eyes.

Just as dinosaur bones are found
buried in rock strata,
we discover a love as old as time.

Like Gregor Mendel's
cross-pollinated peas,
our love is expressed in varied colors.

Just as Leeuwenhoek found the miracle
of microscopic life in pond water,
we find life's wonders in ordinary things.

As cosmonaut Valentina Tereshkova
explored outer space,
we explore the inner spaces of our minds.

Like the "Forty-Niners"
mining for gold in California,
we find treasures of the heart.

As Gandhi changed the world
through nonviolent means,
we live in peace.

Like Jacques Cousteau,
diving deep into the oceans,
we explore the depths of feeling.

As Sir Edmund Hillary's expedition
climbed to the peak of Everest,
we climb the heights of inspiration.

Even as Pompeii was buried by Vesuvius,
we will soon be buried.
I hope, when we are discovered
under the ash and lava,
I will still be holding your hand.

Every Precious Day

Sunny days, dark days...
we're growing old together
every precious day.

You are intellect,
ethics, affection, passion,
thoughtfulness, and joy!

Magic of the moon,
Venus, Mars, and all the stars...
sunshine of your smile.

Wherever I go,
my thoughts are always with you...
Can't wait to come home!

Presence

Present with me
or absent from me,
you are always in my thoughts.
However long I may live,
I will always feel you near.

A Desert Rose

Our little world envelops us in love,
transcending chaos that surrounds us now,
safe haven from Earth's dark duplicity,
a green oasis, peace in desert heat.

Affection in your eyes, my hand in yours,
a gentle word, a loving touch...encouragement
along our earthly path's uncertainties.
Your inner strength sustains my fainting heart.

When threats of war surround on every side...
vile pestilence, pollution, and unrest,
ambition fades, possessions matter less,
but love endures, a desert rose.

Love Flourishes

Timeless memories,
shared hopes for our tomorrows.
We live in the now.

Our energy wanes.
Wit is replaced by wisdom.
Our love flourishes.

Love lights the twilight.
In winter's chill, we are warmed
by each other's gaze.

Oblivion Can Wait

Wakeful in the dim light
and stillness of morning, I lie beside you,
listening to your breathing, holding your hand.
You fall asleep; warm and drowsy, I doze.

I dream that you take my hand.
Together we rise toward peaceful oblivion...
I awaken suddenly...Not today!
Today, the cardinals sing their cheery songs.

Today, the grass is green.
In anticipation of sunrise, ruellias open,
glowing purple in the golden light.
Today, the sun shines.

I drink my tea and write.
Enjoy your dreams, but when you wake,
we will spend the day together.
Today belongs to us...Oblivion can wait!

FAMILY

My Forebears

I long to call you,
Grandma, Grandpa, Mom, and Dad,
when I have good news.

I long to call you,
and hear you say one more time,
"I'm so proud of you!"

I wish I could tell you, "Thanks
for helping me on my way!"

Cactus–Tailed Cat

In 1936, kids were talking in Sunday school:
Hey, did you hear about Harvey?
You mean that guy who always plays the fool?
It's hepatitis! He's at Wheeling Mercy!

Oh, Wow! I didn't know that he was sick!
They think he could die. We might lose a friend.
We'll cheer Harvey up. Think of something quick!
A dozen roses would be nice to send.

The Sunday school class wanted to be kind...
Roses were too expensive, it was clear.
A cat with a cactus tail...What a find!
What a perfect gift to bring Harvey cheer!

Harvey, my dad, was too stubborn to die!
Fifteen-year-old Harvey dodged tragedy.
The cactus-tailed cat was the reason why
they joined the Church...Harvey's whole family!

Harvey became a Methodist preacher,
devoted to service for fifty years.
He was a storyteller and teacher.
He visited the sick and calmed their fears.

Grandma gave the cactus-tailed cat to me,
the cat that changed the family's way of living.
Now it's my daughter Ellen's cat, a legacy
that honors Ellen's life of service and giving.

Mother

Mother
is proud of you
for every step you take,
picks you up every time you fall,
cheers you on again and again,
and builds your confidence
to walk alone...
She's proud!

Mother
hears your first word,
listens to all your dreams,
gives advice, knowing that someday,
you will surely recall
what Mother said...
She hears!

Mother
sees potential
when those around you doubt,
has high hopes for you in tough times,
even when you give up.
Always loves you...
Always!

The $5 Challenge

I had heard the stories as a child...
of Dad skipping school and running wild...
breaking the ice to go for a swim.
Scents of skunk-trapping emanating from him...

Sent home or banished to the hall.
Given his grades for playing basketball.
Joined the Navy by lying about his age.
Used the GI Bill to go to college.

Dad wasn't much help with study skills,
but he gave me an incentive of a five-dollar-bill
for earning straight "A"s, a perfect report card.
In my sophomore year, I tried really hard!

By dropping my hated typing class,
I thought I could earn all "A" s at last!
But the honor roll with a "B" or two
seemed to be the best that I could do.

The next two years, until graduation,
I focused on directing my own education.
I abandoned chasing grades...no "busy work" for me!
There were books to read as far as the eye could see!

After that, I took art class seriously
and sketched my teacher in trigonometry...
Like my father before me, banished to the hall,
I read a book and didn't mind at all.

I was multitasking in trigonometry...
Figuring that out, my teacher tolerated me!
Moved to the back of the class, not banished to the hall...
I sat drawing, learning, and having a ball!

My history teacher was a boring jock!
Outline the chapter? I think he was in shock;
my outline was heads and subheads. My grades slid,
but I got an education despite the rude things I did!

No "busy work" copying sentences in grammar...
Zeros hurt my grades, but it didn't matter...
I scored high on tests, so my grades were okay.
No offense, teachers...just trying to find my way!

Married at eighteen, then job and family.
Night school part-time at twenty-six...I was ready!
At the beginning of each quarter, I always asked,
"What do I have to do to get an "A" in your class?

After all the drama, I finally had my four-point-oh!
Dad's offer had expired...five dollars was a "no show!"
At forty, I graduated and consecutively
started teaching and earning my master's degree.

Like my father before me, I say, "Don't do as I do!"
Educating yourself is essential, but grades matter too!
Dad went back to school after I was grown.
He earned five doctorates...Who could have known?

Honeybunch & Sunshine

Babysitter's cat
had kittens. Wow! Honeybunch
was so excited!

Calico kitten,
Sunshine was a birthday gift...
Honeybunch was three.

Small girl and kitten...
Honeybunch and her Sunshine
became best of friends.

Sunshine was chummy...
swatting and chasing cat toys,
purring and snuggling.

Hiking through the woods,
Sunshine walked with Honeybunch
down to the river.

Cuddled in slumber,
Honeybunch and Sunshine
roamed the land of dreams.

Honeybunch grew up,
Sunshine lived for thirteen years...
They were lifelong friends.

Barney, the Purple Dinosaur

They came to Florida, Katey and her brother,
leaving behind Russia's snowy weather.
Friends and neighbors sent gifts of welcome.
Hanukkah and Christmas gifts filled our home.

That January, when Katey turned five,
a book was the gift that we planned to give.
On Katey's birthday, when Papa came home,
the well-laid birthday plans all came undone.

When Papa came in, Katey was overjoyed.
Between Papa's feet was a Barney toy.
From the wheelchair, Barney saw his new place.
A gigantic grin spread over Papa's face!

When Katey kissed Barney's purple cheek,
the talking dinosaur began to speak.
In his goofy voice, Barney sang, "I love you..."
Undeniably, Katey loved him too!

We lost Papa six years later in January,
weeks before Katey's eleventh birthday.
Barney lived with Katey for twenty-three years.
Barney's tragic demise left Katey in tears.

One year, shopping on Amazon,
I found Katey's Christmas present, a Barney clone!
Barney now lives in Texas, where he'll say,
"I love you," to Katey every day!

NOSTALGIA

Barefoot

Bright spring afternoon,
wading barefoot in the creek,
scooping up tadpoles.

Warm summer evening,
running barefoot through the grass,
fireflies in a jar.

Blue-sky autumn day,
playing barefoot in leaf piles,
watching geese fly south.

Cold winter morning,
barefoot in new-fallen snow...
screaming and laughing!

Hometown Parade

Oh, to stand again on a tree-lined street
in 1956 on a summer day!
My joy would surely be complete
when the high school band began to play.

Majorettes in their tasseled boots,
cute short skirts, and pony-tailed hair
march and twirl amid claps and whoops
and toss their batons in the air.

The high school band marches along,
all spiffy uniforms and shiny brass,
playing a medley of marching songs.
The crowd applauds them as they pass.

Little kids march in place,
mimicking their high-school stars.
As mostly harmonious notes fade away,
we spot big-finned convertible cars...

Beauty queens, regal on Chrysler thrones...
strapless gowns, skirts like fluffy clouds,
ruby-lipped smiles and rhinestone crowns,
waving at whistling, cheering crowds.

Veterans of Korea and World War Two,
in uniforms of army, navy, and marines,
march behind the red, white, and blue...
Faded dreams of glory, old battle scenes.

The children in town are invited
to walk in the parade with their pets.
They come down the street excited,
dogs wearing ribbons around their necks.

Farm wagon floats are dandy,
transformed with crepe paper festoons.
Business floats are throwing candy.
Church choirs sing patriotic tunes.

4-H kids perch on straw bales.
Forest Service float features Smokey Bear.
Jonah sits near a crepe paper whale.
Prize-winning floats created with care!

Shriners maneuver tiny cars around.
Arabian horses prance in fancy gear.
Volunteer firemen are heroes in our town.
Siren wailing...Fire truck's finally here!

I'd like to listen again to a high school band
on a blissful sunny day
with a frosty, five-cent coke in my hand.
Reliving 1956, I'd pass the time away!

Sledding

Saturday morning...soup in the crockpot,
wholegrain bread rising, birdseed scattered
on the snowy porch. Cat at the window
watching cardinals, jays, and finches!

Sunday afternoon...packing a picnic,
dressed in long johns, boots and mittens.
Daughter excited! Driving up the mountain
to George Washington National Forest.

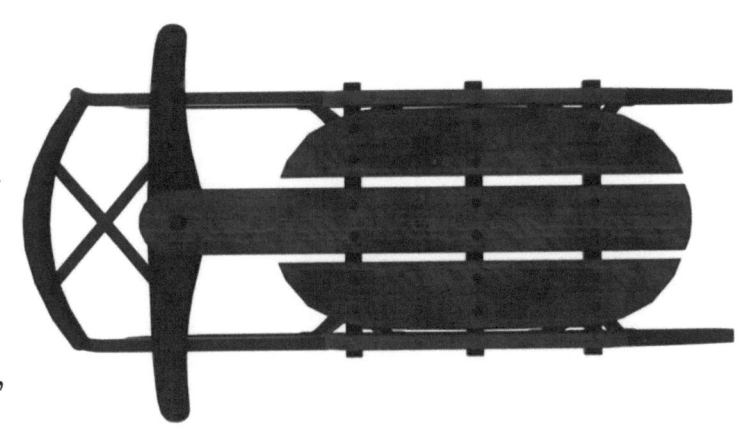

Building a fire, soup pot on the grill.
Sledding downhill, trudging uphill.
Sledding down again, cheeks red with cold,
ice-matted sleeves, jeans wet at the knees.

Steaming mugs of homemade soup,
homemade wholegrain bread.
Sitting, tired and happy at a picnic table,
laughing, talking...making memories!

Blue & White Mugs

Blue and white souvenir mugs
in our Miami Beach drug store...
art deco and wildlife scenes...
I bought four!

The kids grew; we planned to travel...
Kids wanted to help push Dad's chair.
Mom looked forward to collecting
blue and white mugs from everywhere!

A three-generation Caribbean cruise...
Dad's last-minute illness caused cancellation.
We scheduled a Caribbean cruise
that year for our family vacation.

I spent a night in the hospital with Dad...
They failed to draw blood despite many tries.
Dad checked himself out before daybreak.
We drove to the beach to watch the sun rise.

Then we went home to pack our bags
for the final voyage of the Norway...
Mom, dad, and kids sailed that afternoon.
We had decided to "seize the day!"

We snorkeled, following colorful fish,
explored quaint tropical islands,
listened to steel bands, went to shows...
and we bought a mug, as I had planned.

Dad died within the year. I put the
Caribbean mug where it wouldn't break,
fragile, precious souvenir of the
only family cruise we would ever take.

Years later, I retired to the Gulf Coast.
Just one Miami Beach mug remained
when we moved to our present house.
I thought about putting that mug away.

I chose to enjoy both mugs fearlessly.
When the Miami Beach mug broke,
I gave the last mug to my daughter, Katey,
souvenir of the family cruise we took.

Candy Box

A gold foil candy box
was my treasure chest.
Candy was a sweet gift,
but the box was the best!

I filled it with love letters
and cherished photos
collected over a period
of five years or so.

I carried the box around
for more than fifty years.
One year, the box fell apart;
I didn't shed any tears.

I looked at the photos,
read the letters once more,
put them all in the trash,
and walked out the door.

We moved to our new house,
vowing we'd never move again.
Mementos fade, but the photos and
letters are burned on my brain.

I remember a boy with
slicked-back hair and crooked grin,
and a handsome football player
who wanted me to marry him.

I remember a fearless boy
who helped me learn to drive
and several others
who passed through my life.

I put the box away
when I married at eighteen...
Now the mementos are gone,
but the memories remain.

MOTHER NATURE

Morning Fog

Chill early morning.
Fog hovers over the lake...
soft, enveloping,
a cocoon of solitude
gives birth to glorious day!

Mountain Memories

An antlered deer bounds to sheltering trees.
A doe and spotted fawn graze lush meadows.
Seeking sylvan sanctuaries of peace
in our youth, we find the hidden hollows.

We view mountain vistas in morning mist,
green valleys and winding river below.
Ravens glide on updrafts in sky-blue bliss,
silent above an ancient hemlock grove.

We descend a steep trail beside a stream;
water music echoes through the forest.
At journey's end, the waterfall of dreams
is singing the "Hallelujah Chorus!"

My dreams play reruns of old memories
of blue mountains and green river valleys.

Swimming with Manatees

During the summer, manatees
wander widely in warm seas.
In winter, manatees hold jamborees
in hot springs near seventy degrees.

Hundreds of manatees socialize in Kings Bay
near Three Sisters Springs on November days.
Manatees enjoy each other's company...
They don't need to compete for territory.

Vegetarians, they live on sea grass...
How peacefully, how gracefully their days pass!
Nursing calves swim beside their mothers.
They have no predators, no fear of others.

Though manatees bear the scars
of encounters with boat propellers,
they still seek humans as their playmates.
Snuggles and belly rubs they celebrate.

As I climbed down the boat ladder,
a manatee waited for me in the water.
A thousand pounds of curiosity
and kind manatee eyes greeted me.

The moment we came face to face,
I knew there was hope for the human race.
At that moment, it became clear to me
that people could learn from manatees.

How happy life would be
if we could live in harmony
with nature and our fellow creatures.
Manatees are charming teachers!

Of the Water

We exist, submerged
in the womb, that inner sea,
until our first breath.

In our veins flows blood
with the sea's salinity...
seas...where life began.

Water in our cells,
water in our mother's milk,
water in our tears.

We are of water...
bodies more than half water.
Water sustains us.

Water in the clouds,
streams, rivers, lakes, seas, oceans,
aquifers, ice caps.

Beauty of water
soothes our spirits, inspires us...
Water refreshes.

Every living thing on Earth
needs clean, life-giving water.

Gopher Tortoise

"Hey there, you carrying
the tortoise! Hello!"
The boy was walking
toward the Gulf of Mexico.

"Don't put that tortoise
in the water, please!
It's not a sea turtle
that travels the seas!"

"That's a gopher tortoise,
endangered, protected by law."
"I didn't know," replied the boy.
"It's the first one I ever saw!"

The boy put the tortoise
gently down on the sand,
and it crawled very slowly
up the beach to dry land.

I wish I had said, "Read about
gopher tortoises in Wikipedia,
and tell your friends back home
about meeting one in Florida."

Little Human vs. Global Destruction

Global Destruction, a villain
about as bad as they come,
believed his evil takeover plan
was too big to be undone.

"What do I care, Little Human,
for your miniscule potential?
Do what little you can;
it's quite inconsequential!"

Joy sprang like a weed
in the Little Human's heart.
He knew humans could succeed
if they all did their part!

Save Mother Earth!

Governmental delegates, scientists,
and assorted environmentalists...
many nations sent delegations
to help Mother Earth find salvation!

International scientists all agreed,
"Clean energy is what we need.
Clean up the land, sea, and air.
Protect animal habitats everywhere."

Then the governmental delegates,
after prolonged debates,
decreed, "We must enact regulations
to be strictly enforced by all nations."

Environmentalists were next to speak:
"Your governmental coercion plan is very weak!
We must set hearts and minds on fire...
educate and motivate, persuade and inspire!"

Suddenly, youthful eco-activists appeared,
determined to make their message heard.
"The future belongs to us!" they chanted.
Protest signs proclaimed what they wanted.

"Save the Rainforest! Clean up the Sea!
Organic food! Renewable Energy!
Save Wildlife Habitats! War is an Outrage!
Protect Polar Bears! Lower the Voting Age!"

Young speakers took the microphone.
They said, "No group of experts can work alone.
Scientists, governments, and environmentalists must
work together to earn our trust."

"The future belongs to us! We take a stand...
The children of the world demand...
Stop your games and endless debate,
and save Mother Earth before it's too late!"

Walk with Me

My heart is in the mountains.
My feet are in the sea.
My head is in the clouds,
my arms around a tree.

We can talk with the animals...
Come, walk the world with me!

Photo Credits

Front Cover Asad, Pexels

Dedication Cheryl Batavia

Transitions Pexels-Pixabay
Identity Crisis shot-by-ireland, Unsplash
This Little Boat Joakim Honkasalo, Unsplash
Among Friends Zachary Nelson, Unsplash
Message in a Bottle Lakshya Thakur, Unsplash
I Am the Moment Christopher Farrugia, Unsplash
I Am the Moment Ricardo Braham, Unsplash

Summer Rain Jonathan Petit, Unsplash
Just the Two of Us Bram, Adobe Stock
Great Discoveries of Love Denise Jones, Unsplash
A Desert Rose Joao Guilherme Soares Dias, Unsplash
Love Flourishes Aaron Doucett, Unsplash

My Forebears Alena Darmel, Pexels
Cactus-Tailed Cat Eve Ellen Maher
The $5 Challenge Joseph Greve, Unsplash
The $5 Challenge Karolina Grabowska, Pexels
Honeybunch & Sunshine H.P. Koch, Unsplash
Barney, the Purple Dinosaur Katey Batavia

Barefoot Olia Danilevich, Pexels
Hometown Parade Bercerra Govea, Pexels
Hometown Parade firetruck, Pixabay
Sledding sled, Pixabay
Blue and White Mugs Cheryl Batavia

Morning Fog Enrique Meseguer, Pixabay
Mountain Memories Guy Sagi, Adobe Stock
Swimming with Manatees Janos, Adobe Stock
Of the Water Eve Ellen Maher
Gopher Tortoise Dawn McDonald, Unsplash
Save Mother Earth Mika Baumeister, Unsplash
Walk with Me Dennis Eusebio, Unsplash

Back Cover Stephanie Snow Photography